ISLE OF MAN
ACU Official
Raceguide

TT'82

TT
1999

THE WORLD'S MOST IMPORTANT

A WORLD CHAMPIONSHIP MEETING
OFFICIAL PROGRAMME AND GUIDE
1966

DUNLOP
the best things on two wheels
AGAIN PROVED IN THE 1965 TT · 1st, 2nd and 3rd IN ALL EVENTS

Published by R&S Productions Ltd.
Text by Rennie Scaysbrook. Illustrations by Genivieve LeDuc.
renniescaysbrook.com

ISBN 979-8-9851195-1-0

Summary: Steve Hislop and Carl Fogarty participate in the 1992 Isle of Man Senior TT, producing a race that has gone down in memory as one of the greatest ever held on the Isle of Man.

Special thanks to Peter Duke at Duke Video, David Goldman at Gold & Goose Photography, Rob McElnea, Paul Phillips and all the staff at the Isle of Man TT, Mark Huckerby Photography, Jim and Sue Scaysbrook, Simon Hallam for being the best mate anyone could ask for, and Annabelle and Harvey Scaysbrook for providing the inspiration for this book.

RACE
OF THE
TITANS

Researched and written by
Rennie Scaysbrook

Illustrated by
Genivieve Le Duc

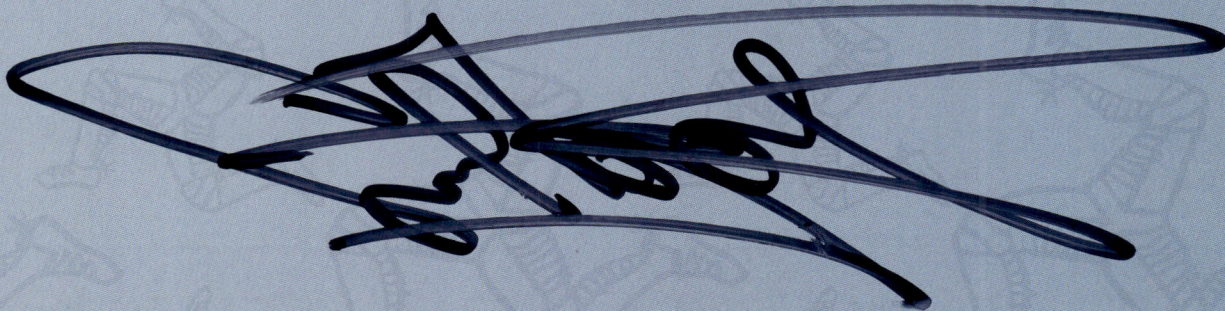

The Isle of Man held its first Tourist Trophy (TT) motorcycle race in 1907 and it quickly became the most famous event of its kind anywhere in the world.

At an incredible 37.73 miles long, the TT Mountain Course is a mythical, magical place. This is a real roads racetrack that is run through towns, past houses and schools and around the island's iconic Snaefell mountain.

Riders reach speeds over 200 mph on the TT Mountain Course. It is a circuit only the very bravest dare to take on.

On 6 June 1992, on this little island in the middle of the Irish Sea, a TT race was held that was so fast and so spectacular, it would transform its two starring riders, Steve Hislop and Carl Fogarty, into TT legends.

Quarry Bends

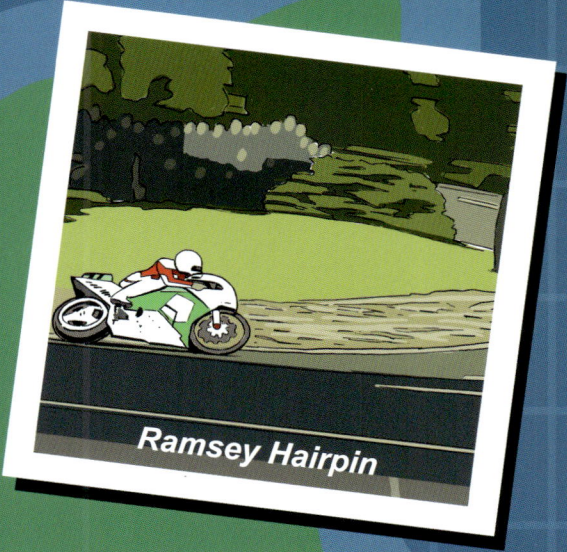

Ramsey Hairpin

Quarry Bends

Ramsey Hairpin

Kirk Michael

Kirk Michael

The Bungalow

The Bungalow

Creg-ny-Baa

Bray Hill

Bray Hill

Start/Finish

Creg-ny-Baa

Scotland's Steve Hislop was a quiet man, but his gentle demeanour belied a speed few could match at the Isle of Man TT.

By 1992, Hislop was already an eight-time TT winner, making him one of the most successful TT riders of all time.

That year, the young Hislop made it his mission to win the British Superbike Championship. However, it wasn't to be. Hislop's British championship season did not go as planned and it looked like he might be out of the Isle of Man TT, too.

But then, a Norton became available.

1989 Formula One TT

1987 Formula 2 TT

1989 Formula One TT

Steve Hislop had an idea.
He needed a competitive motorcycle to bring in some much needed prize money, and legendary British brand Norton had an ace up its sleeve with its revolutionary NRS 588 rotary-engined racer. Fearsomely fast and difficult to ride, the Norton NRS 588 was an angry animal of a motorcycle.

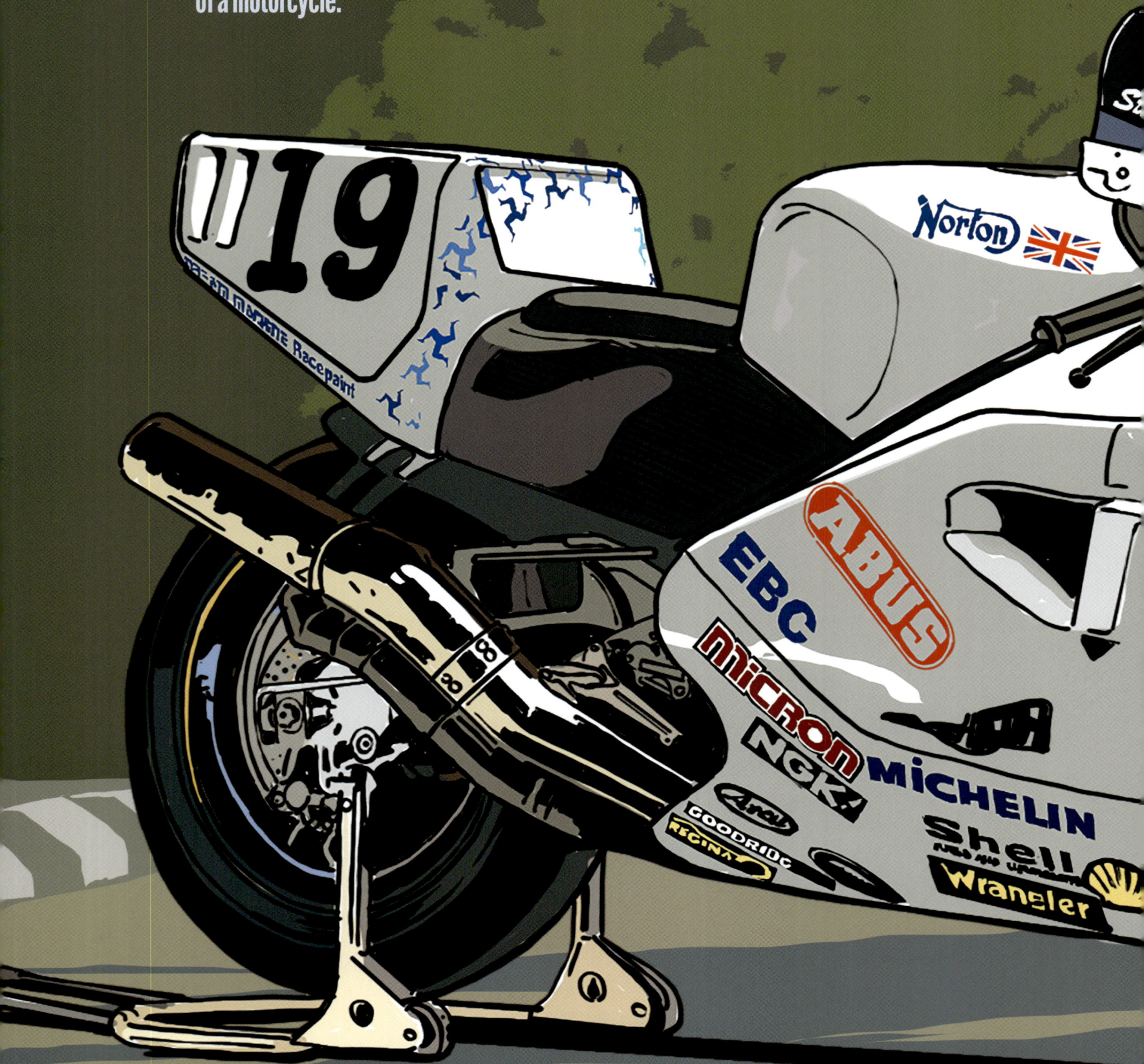

Hislop decided to lease the Norton NRS 588 for the 1992 Isle of Man TT and the team was backed by Hislop's personal sponsor ABUS, the beautiful all-white paint scheme seeing Hislop's Norton christened, The White Charger. Hislop knew it would take a special rider to tame the Norton in what he said at the time would be his last Isle of Man TT meeting.

Norton NRS 588

Engine: Twin-rotor rotary

Capacity: 588 cc

Power: 135 horsepower

Transmission: Six speed

Chassis: Aluminium twin-spar

Weight: 135 kg/297 lb (without fuel)

Carl Fogarty was the great hope for a British world champion in the early 1990s.
The boy from Blackburn had done his time at the Isle of Man with three TT wins around the Mountain
Course by 1992.
Fogarty was looking for new challenges and he had just taken his first win in the World Superbike
Championship at Donington Park in the UK on a Ducati that he funded himself.

However, racing World Superbike on your own is very expensive and the chance to
ride a Yamaha FZR750R OW01 meant a TT payday was now on offer that Fogarty could not afford to
turn down. Fogarty thus saddled up on the Yamaha with sponsorship from Loctite, which gave the
machine its distinctive red and white colour scheme.

1990 Formula One TT

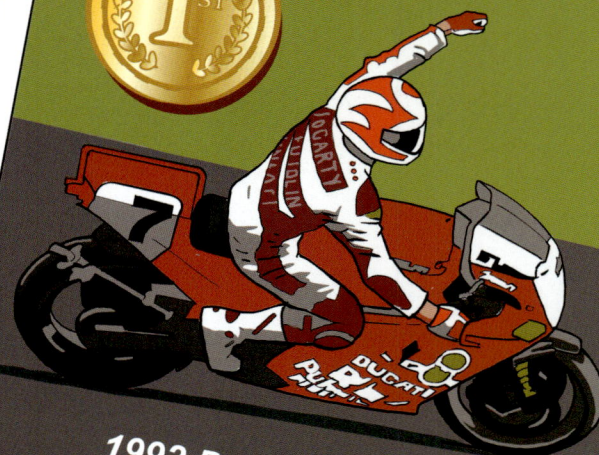

1992 Donington Park
World Superbike

1989 Production
750 cc TT

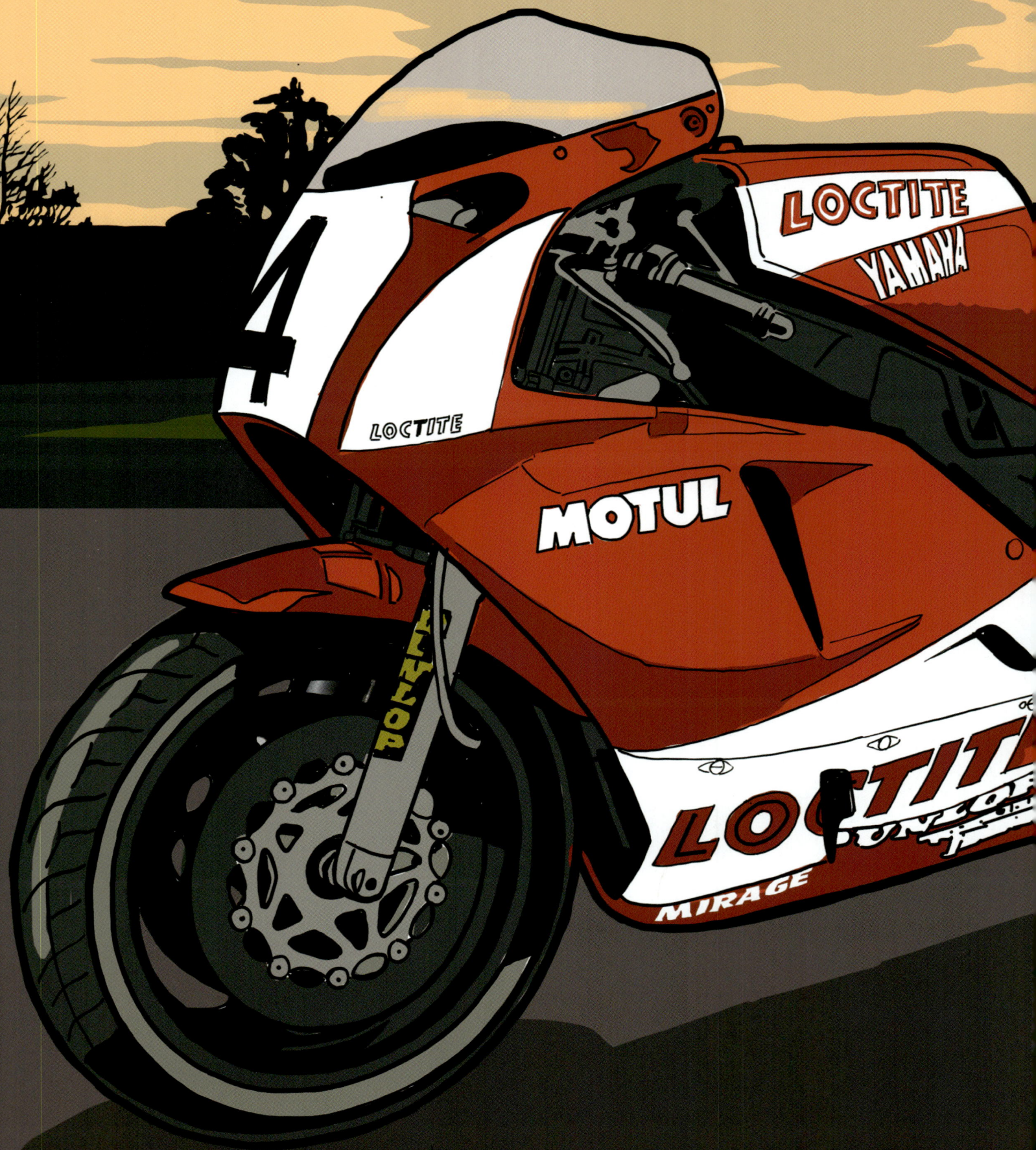

The Yamaha FZR750R OW01 was one of the finest superbikes ever created by Japanese company Yamaha.

The world first laid eyes on the four-cylinder OW01 in 1989 and Carl Fogarty's racer produced a mega 140 horsepower.

The Yamaha was perfectly suited to the regular short circuits normally found around the world but the super high-speed nature of the TT course meant it was slightly slower than Hislop's fast but fragile Norton.

1992 was going to be Carl's last year at the TT—his dream was to race in the World Superbike Championship—but he wanted to finish his TT career in style by standing on the top step of the podium.

Yamaha FZR750R OW01

Engine: Four-cylinder, four-stroke

Capacity: 749 cc

Power: 140 horsepower

Transmission: Six speed

Chassis: Aluminium twin-spar

Weight: 187 kg/412 lb (without fuel)

What is a rotary engine?

A rotary engine spins a single shaft with a triangular-shaped rotor on one end. There are three chambers surrounding the rotor. The spinning rotor draws air and fuel into the first chamber, compresses and fires it in the second chamber, and spits out the exhaust gases in the third chamber. A rotary engine is light and powerful but burns lots of fuel and can run very hot. However, it does make an awesome, raspy noise on full throttle.

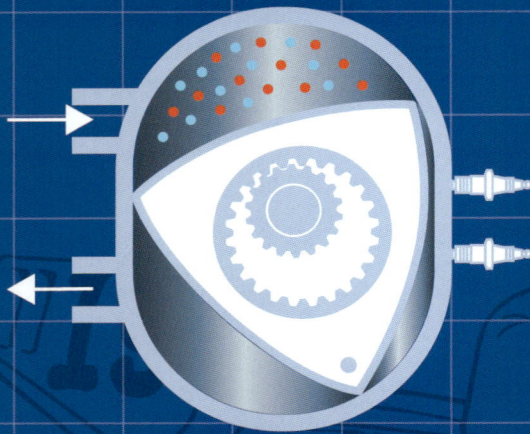

Intake

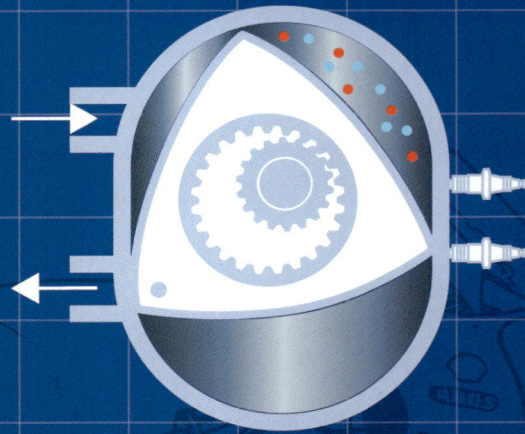

Compression

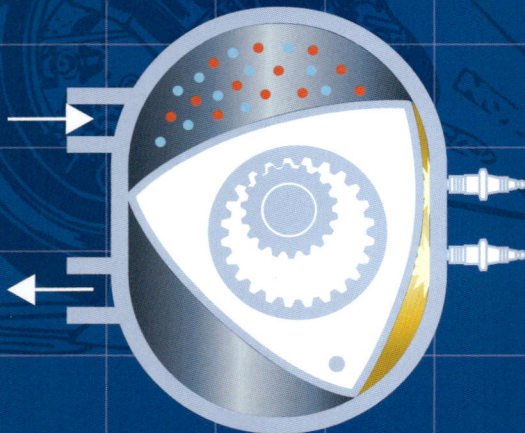

Power

Exhaust

What is a four-stroke piston engine ?

In a four-stroke piston engine, the air and fuel mixture is drawn into the engine during the intake stroke. The compression stroke sees the crankshaft push the connecting rod and piston up, compressing the mixture, which is then ignited on the power stroke. Finally, the spent gasses are sent out of the engine during the exhaust stroke. A four-cylinder piston engine has an incredible sound, although it is very different to that of a rotary.

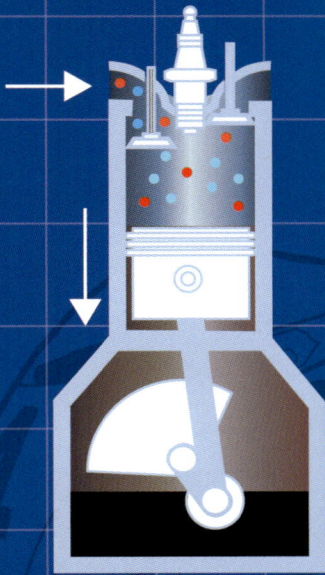

Intake

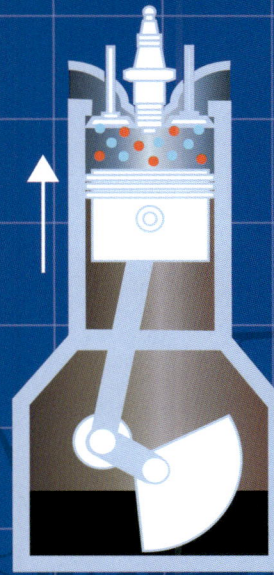

Compression

Power

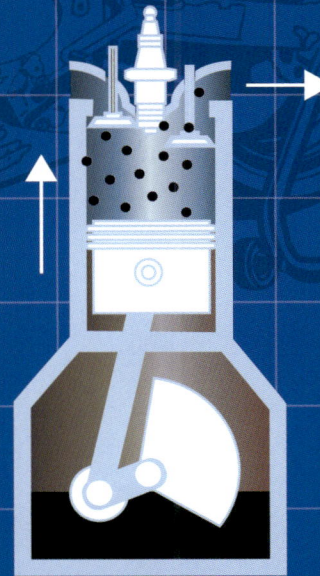

Exhaust

Although there were eight races scheduled for the 1992 Isle of Man TT,
the world's eyes were focused on the two races that contained the most powerful bikes:
the Formula One TT and the oldest motorcycle race in the world, the Senior TT.

The first event of the 1992 Isle of Man TT was the Formula One race and **Carl Fogarty asserted his authority.** The Briton and his flying Yamaha were way out in front until his gearbox destroyed itself at The Bungalow on the fifth lap, leaving Fogarty devastated but determined on righting the wrong in the Senior TT later that week.

The Formula One TT was won by a young **Phillip McCallen**. He got to spray the winner's champagne for the very first time after finishing ahead of Hislop and third-placed Joey Dunlop.

TT FORMULA ONE WINNER

However, **heat from the Norton's rotary engine was proving problematic.** Hislop's teammate, Robert Dunlop, retired from the Formula One TT with a seized engine and so the Norton team removed the front wheel guard and created extra vents in the bodywork to get more airflow around the engine. The mechanics also changed each Norton's carburettor jetting to lower the engine temperature and help the machines last the six laps of the Senior TT.

Friday, 6 June 1992, dawned clear and cool over Douglas Promenade on the Isle of Man. Rays of perfect sunshine coated the TT Mountain Course, signalling the best possible conditions for the race everyone wanted to win—the Senior TT.

Nervous tension filled the air as riders checked and rechecked their bikes in an effort to calm their minds before taking on the most treacherous racetrack in the world.

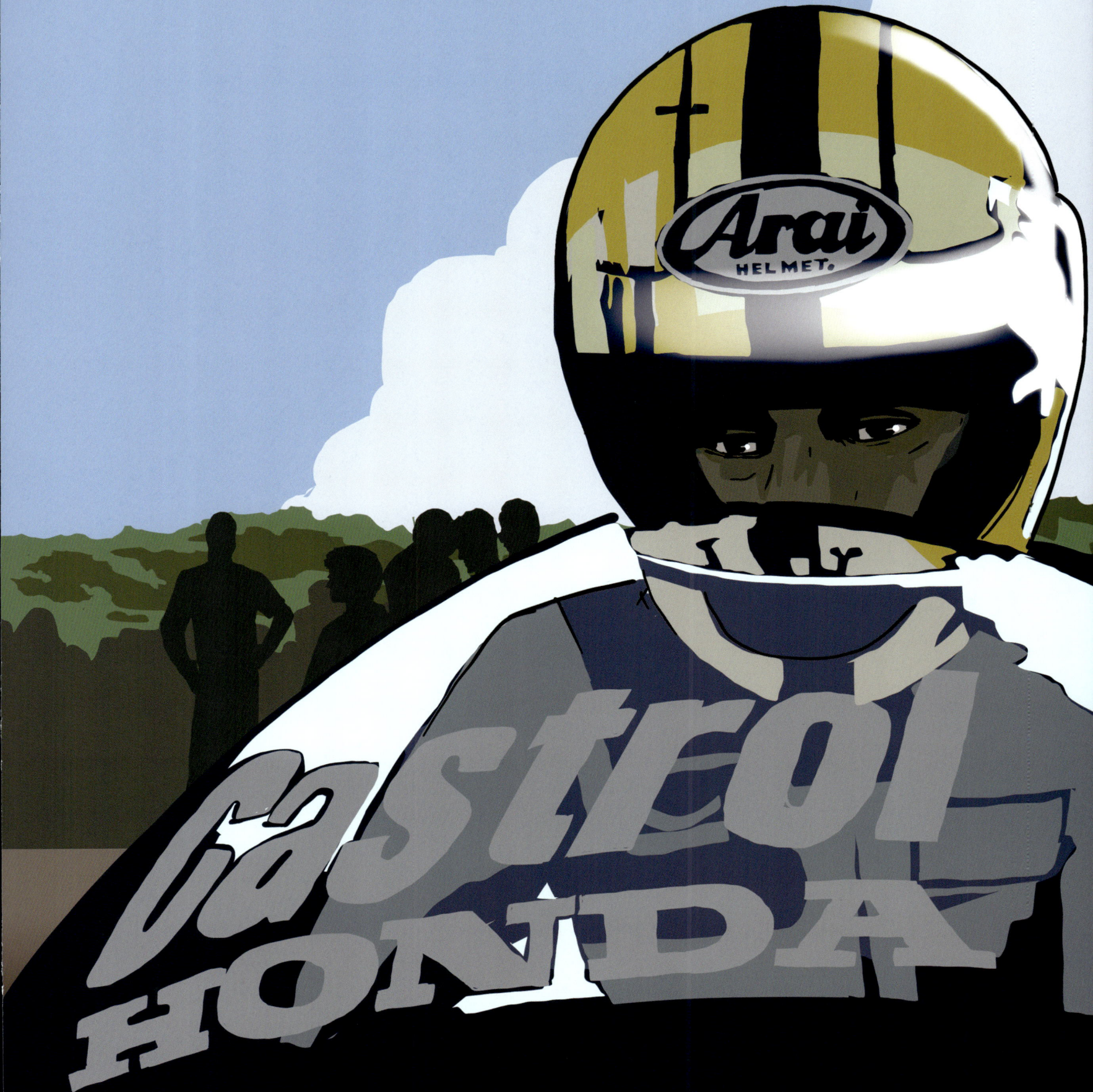

Ahead lay six laps and 226 miles of white-knuckle racing around the TT Mountain Course.

Steve Hislop and the Norton NRS 588 rode into the history books and bettered Carl Fogarty by only 4.4 seconds after one hour and fifty-two minutes of intense competition to win the 1992 Isle of Man Senior TT!

Fogarty had tried all he knew to defeat Hislop and set a new lap record of 123.61 mph, a mark that would not be beaten for an incredible seven years. Hislop and Fogarty laughed as they shared the podium with third-placed Robert Dunlop and took in the cheers of the adoring crowd.

Little did they know, but Carl Fogarty and Steve Hislop had just staged one of the greatest Isle of Man TT races in history.

Carl Fogarty never did return to the Isle of Man TT.

True to his word, Fogarty put everything into his World Superbike career, landing a factory Ducati ride for 1993 and finishing second to American Kawasaki rider Scott Russell.

The 1994 season saw Carl Fogarty come into his own. On the legendary Ducati 916, Fogarty took his and Britain's first World Superbike title. He repeated the feat in 1995, then again in 1998 and 1999.

Carl Fogarty retired from motorcycle racing in 2000.

Carl Fogarty throws the front wheel in the air at Phillip Island in Australia.

Photography by Gold & Goose

Steve Hislop on the gas as he crests The Mountain at Cadwell Park in the UK.

Isle of Man TT racing motorcycles through the ages

1900s
Charlie Collier, 3.5 hp Matchless 500

1910s
Frank Applebee, 3.5 hp Scott 500

1920s
Stanley Woods, Norton ES2

1930s
Freddie Frith, Norton Manx 500